St. Neots
in old picture postcards volume 1

door R.E. Young

European Library ZALTBOMMEL/THE NETHERLANDS

Views of St. Neots, Eynesbury, Eaton Socon and Eaton Ford taken between 1880 and 1930 and reproduced from items in the collections of L.C. Forscutt and D.J. Wills.

GB ISBN 90 288 2581 9

© 1983 European Library – Zaltbommel/The Netherlands

Fifth edition, 1997: reprint of the original edition of 1983.

INTRODUCTION

St. Neots is a town of about 22,000 inhabitants, situated at a crossing of the River Ouse. It was in Huntingdonshire until that county was abolished in 1972 and it is now part of Cambridgeshire. The town includes Eynesbury, which was also in Huntingdonshire, and Eaton Socon and Eaton Ford which originally belonged to Bedfordshire. A main road from Cambridge passes through the town from east to west and over the river bridge, and to the west of the river is the A 1, the route between London and the North of England.

The town takes its name from a Saxon Saint who lived and died in Cornwall in the 9th century and who probably had no connections with Huntingdonshire during his lifetime. A small monastery dedicated to Saint Neot was established by an Anglo-Saxon Earl in the parish of Eynesbury in the 10th century. The Normans took it over and rebuilt it on a site near the river and it became a Priory under the authority of the Abbey of Bec in France. A market place was set out beside the Priory and a community rapidly grew up around it in the Middle Ages, catering for market traders, local farmers and the many pilgrims who visited the Priory to see the bones of the Saint. By the end of the 12th century 'Saint Neot's town' had outstripped its parent settlement at Eynesbury and had acquired separate parish status.

Although all trace of the Priory and its buildings disappeared within a few years of the Dissolution of the Monasteries in the 16th century, St. Neots continued to thrive as a market centre throughout the next 300 years. Many of the buildings round the Market Square were originally 17th and 18th century merchants' houses with yards running back to the river and its tributary. Goods and raw materials were transported by water until the beginning of this century. In the late 18th and early 19th centuries the stage-coaches brought more trade to the town, particularly Eaton Socon which was on a very busy main route.

With the passing of the coaching era Eaton suffered a slight decline, but St. Neots had the advantage of a railway link with London and its own station after 1850. During the late 19th century several new roads were constructed at St. Neots and Eynesbury and houses were built along them, large detached residences for the middle classes and terraces of cottages for the 'artisans'. A number of old thatched cottages were demolished between 1880 and 1910, and shops and business premises in the town centre were altered or rebuilt.

For the residents of the town in the late 19th and early 20th centuries life was very different from today. As many of the pictures in this book will show, the pace of life was much slower and there were few traffic problems. The leisurely speed of horse-drawn carriages and carts caused no hazards for pedestrians and local children had no qualms about playing games in the street. The roads themselves were poorly surfaced with gravel chippings until the first asphalt was laid in 1904, and only the main roads had street lamps powered by gas.

The principal occupations of the inhabitants of St. Neots at that time were agriculture, commerce and domestic service, with a number of people also working at the Paper Mills and a few employed at Day's Brewery. Most people were in employment but for the paupers of the town and the surrounding villages there was a Union Workhouse at Eaton Ford. The dominant personality in the town was George Fydell Rowley who lived at Priory Hill House and was Lord of the Manor from 1902.

A large area of Common Land at St. Neots provided recreation space for the townspeople as well as grazing for the cattle of the Common Rights holders, and games of cricket, football and golf were regularly played there. There was bathing from the bank of the meadow in the summer and skating on the frozen meadow in the winter. The river was the focus of a great deal of activity during the summer months, with rowing boats for the sportsmen and houseboats for the less energetic. At certain times there were Feasts and Fairs. St. Neots held four Fairs, one of which was a Statute Fair at which labourers presented themselves for hire, and both Eynesbury and St. Neots conducted ceremonies on May Day which involved small children parading a floral garland through the streets, collecting money. Eaton Socon was famous for its Maypole Dancing, the maypole being a permanent feature on the Green until it was blown down in a gale in 1915.

After World War One there was some rebuilding in the town, but the major expansion took place after World War Two. The local Council entered into a London Overspill agreement under which families from the city moved to St. Neots and small businesses also came to provide employment. New housing estates grew up all around, covering land that had been farmland for centuries, and eventually merging the original four areas of St. Neots, Eynesbury, Eaton Ford and Eaton Socon into one large conurbation. Commercial premises in the town centre were once again rebuilt in many cases and small industrial estates were developed at St. Neots and Eaton.

The pictures in this book portray the town as it was before these changes took place. They show a quiet, homely town, unpolluted by the noise and the fumes of cars and heavy lorries, and show a gentler, more placid way of life that has now gone for ever.

1. The life of St. Neots has always revolved around its Market Square. A card postmarked 1909 shows the Square in about 1905. There were no cars or lorries then to endanger pedestrians or pollute the goods displayed on the pavement. The block of buildings facing the camera still showed the shape of the old market courthouse which had once stood there, although part of it had already been altered, housing the St. Neots Advertiser and the London Central Meat Company. The Day column, which now supports only hanging flower baskets, had been fitted with 'incandescent lamps' and a flagpole in 1897, after erection 1822.

2. From the top of a building opposite the photographer took a picture of the north side of the Market Square in 1896 or 1897, at buildings which are not there now, apart from the Cross Keys at the extreme left. In the background, behind Mr. Wright's shop, was the Wesleyan School, built in 1858 and now demolished. The groups of people in the foreground suggest that the picture was taken at a Statute Fair held in September, when labourers came to offer themselves for hire to prospective employers.

Market Square, St Neots

3. This card shows the view looking westwards across the Square towards the river, and it is postmarked 1905. The Angel Inn on the right has long ago disappeared and nearly all the buildings between it and the Cross Keys have been rebuilt. The narrow road leading to the bridge can be seen in the background. On the right of it was a butcher's shop, next to an inn called the Half Moon, later renamed The Bridge Hotel.

4. A view from slightly further east, looking in the same direction, shows Barrett's Victoria House on the corner of New Street, selling men's suits for 12s. 6d. in about 1900. Two doors down was Mr. Boutall, a saddler, and between his premises and the Fox and Hounds Inn, which gave up its licence in 1910, was a narrow alley to Priory Lane. The alley survived the building alterations and a wider version of it is still in use.

5. The north side of the Market Square in 1915, by which time several changes had taken place. New shop-fronts reflected changes of ownership, but the upper floors remained the same in many cases. Teams of heavy horses were pulling the guns of World War One through the streets, watched by local shoppers, and a few residents were getting a grand-stand view from windows above the shops.

6. Another picture, dated about 1916, shows soldiers parading on the Market Square. The men are 'standing easy' which explains the rather untidy ranks. The Half Moon, in the background, had been rebuilt in brick by then, absorbing the butcher's shop on the corner, and would shortly emerge as The Bridge Hotel. There were shops from the Cross Keys to the corner of The Priory as the Arcade was not constructed until 40 years later.

7. The south side of the Square was nearly all residential when this picture was taken in 1904. The house with Sale notices on it had been the birthplace of G.C. Gorham who wrote the first history of St. Neots and Eynesbury, published in 1820. At the time of the sale, on December 8th, 1904, the house was described as having a Brass Foundry at the rear, a previous occupant having been George Bower, an ironfounder. Although shop-fronts now give a different look to these buildings, the old waggon-arches are still there and the house at the left is unchanged.

8. Market Street seen from South Street with the Square beyond in about 1905. On the corner at the left of the picture was the Queens Head public house, delicensed in 1908. The old woman was called Naomi Smith. She was a local gypsy with an unpredictable temper, regarded with some fear by small children. It is said that when she realised that her picture had been taken she threatened to throw a brick through the photographer's shop-window.

9. Mr. Whitmee took over the bakery and shop in South Street shown here in about 1903 and, as his sign recorded, it was 'lately Ekins', several generations of that family having kept it before. This advertising card shows the baker standing proudly in his shop-doorway while two children feast their eyes on the good things in his window. In more recent years the bakery was in the hands of the Shepherd family who continued the long tradition of fine baking.

10. Most of the buildings shown in this picture have been demolished. Taken from a high viewpoint, it shows the Priory Brewery owned by the Day family from 1814 until 1919 when the last member of the family died and the business was sold. It occupied a site north of the Market Square where the Mediaeval Priory of St. Neot stood until the 16th century. Now a community centre overlooks the river and only the Oast House and a small part of the Maltings attached to it have survived.

11. The river and the crossing over it were the reason for the first settlement at St. Neots and the Ouse has always been important to the town, providing a transport route and a source of recreation. In 1889 a severe winter froze the river so completely that the skating and other sports which normally took place on a flooded and frozen meadow were enjoyed on the river itself. In this picture the buildings of the Priory Brewery are on the right.

River from the Bridge, St: Neots

12. Boating was a favourite pastime with residents and visitors alike as this card, post-marked 1906, shows. Mr. Beeson, the proprietor of the Half Moon, hired out boats from the landing stage at the right of this picture. He also owned a bungalow on the river bank beyond the Paper Mills which was rented out to holidaymakers. Regatta Meadow, on the left, was at that time in a semi-natural state, badly drained and subject to flooding each winter.

13. Another view of the frozen Ouse in 1889 shows the scene looking southwards this time towards the town bridge, with the Priory Brewery on the left. At the right is one of the sailing barges which brought raw materials to St. Neots from coastal ports, and transported goods out. It was stuck fast in the ice, providing an adventure playground for a group of local boys.

The Bridge, St. Neots

14. A card posted in 1906 gives a clearer view of the bridge as it looked until the 1960's. The first bridge over the river was a Mediaeval timber one and it was rebuilt in stone in the late 16th or early 17th century, with small arches like the one seen here on the left. The bridge was slightly widened and larger arches were made in later centuries but it still proved impractical for modern traffic and had to be replaced by the present concrete structure.

St. Neots Bridge and River Terrace.

15. A card of about 1910 with a view of the bridge from the other side. The tall chimney of the Brewery spoils an otherwise pleasant scene. The houses of River Terrace, half of which have now been demolished, had private landing stages beside which the owners moored their boats. The red-brick building right of the bridge was the Public Rooms, built in 1853 and knocked down in the 1960's. On the Eaton side of the river the osier beds were marshy and were used only by fishermen before the Riverside Park was laid out.

House Boats on River Ouse, St. Neots.

16. Houseboats were very popular in the early part of this century, as demonstrated by this card, posted in 1906. The boat at the right was called 'Iris'. The bridge is at the extreme left. The tall chimney, since truncated, was attached to the John Bull Mill owned by Paine and Company and in operation until the 1960's in a yard south of St. Neots Market Square.

Bathing Place, St. Neots

17. Bathing was as popular as boating and in 1911, when this card was published, there were two bathing places by the river at St. Neots and one at Eynesbury. This shows the Top Boardings on the banks of Lammas Meadow, near The Lagoons. Bathing was by arrangement with the meadow owners and the holders of Common Rights, the latter having the right to graze cattle there from August to April. The grazing rights have survived but not the bathing place.

18. Leading off St. Neots Market Square is the High Street. It was dominated in this picture by the Corn Exchange on the corner of South Street. The clock was fitted to mark Queen Victoria's Jubilee in 1887 and as Mr. Kirby had left his shop on the New Street corner by 1890, this card dates from 1888 or 1889. In the 1920's the Corn Exchange became a cinema and was rebuilt more recently to become shops and offices. A few doors down the local fire-engine was housed in a building that had once been the 'lock-up' for wrongdoers.

19. This view was taken in about 1895. By then Freeman, Hardy and Willis had taken over Mr. Kirby's shop on the corner of New Street, but the tall building on the right of the High Street, later to accommodate Eastern Gas, was not yet built. Most of the buildings shown here have been rebuilt but the decorative eaves, chimneys and windows of the tall building at the left are still there.

20. The postmark on this card is 1912, and the presence of the Boy Scout confirms that the picture was taken later than 1909. The view is from the north-east corner of the Market Square and the Golden Ball public house appears on the right, its timber-framed plaster encased in brick by then. There is a gas lamp on the pavement. Freeman, Hardy and Willis had completely rebuilt their shop by 1910 and improvements had been made to the roads. The tall cupola of the Corn Exchange towers over the scene.

21. This row of shops on the north side of the High Street included a drapery selling fabrics at 3d. and 6d. a yard when this picture was taken in about 1900. Mr. Norris's shop with the dormer windows and a shop with iron balconies next to the Consumers Tea Company remind us of how the shops must have looked in the 18th century. Both buildings disappeared in the 1960's.

22. The banner records Queen Victoria's second Jubilee in 1897. Flags were displayed on the iron balconies of the shop already mentioned. This view is taken from the opposite direction, looking west, and shows the tall building which later became a gas showroom, next to Mr. Lynn's ironmongery. It is interesting to note that even though the streets were not asphalted, the pavements had stone slabs and there were cobbled gutters.

23. Another celebration took place in 1919, commemorating the end of World War One. A procession of children carried flags down the High Street, accompanied by parents or teachers. The shopfronts had changed by then, but the shop with the iron balconies is recognisable, decked once more with flags. In the foreground the New Inn displayed not only a flag but the symbol of the Cyclists Touring Club.

St. Neots. High Street.

24. This card was posted in 1904 and shows a picture taken about 1900. Ellwoods produced boots and shoes and next to them was the Congregational Church, now the United Reformed Church. The lamp on the pavement by the church railings was first lit on October 15th, 1897. Ellwoods left in 1908 and were replaced by the Westminster Bank who rebuilt the premises in the 1970's. The Dewdrop Inn vanished some time after 1913.

25. This card was issued in about 1900 by Plum's as an advertisement for their shop, which included dining rooms and sold poultry and wine as well as confectionery. The Plum family were said to be descendants of a refugee from the French Revolution. The pretty window boxes overflowing with flowers can also be seen in the previous picture. This shop and the one next to it were rebuilt as Boots the Chemist.

High Street, St. Neots.

26. Looking westwards from The Cross at the eastern end of the High Street, the shopping area looked like this in about 1905. The card is postmarked 1908 but as Ellwoods had moved by then the photograph must have been taken earlier. Mr. Flanders' hairdressing shop with its barbers pole, and the Ship Inn have long since vanished along with nearly every other building seen here.

27. This view of the south side of the High Street is almost unrecognisable as the same area today. Mr. Ennal's wines and spirits shop, in the foreground of this 1890's picture, was later rebuilt as the Royal Oak public house, absorbing the shop next door as well. Behind the brickwork of the building with a jutting-out ground floor there lurked unsuspected the beautiful half-timbering of the now-restored jeweller's shop on the corner of Church Walk.

28. On April 30th, 1908 St. Neots High Street was flooded. Floods were a regular occurrence in the town before improvements to the river and bridge, but the water was usually confined to the Market Square area. As this card shows, the water was deep enough to require plank walkways to the shops, which seems to have amused the people watching from an upper window. At the left the Royal Oak can be seen. Mr. Lynn's shop became a chemist's in recent years, then a boutique.

29. At the extreme eastern end of the High Street, on the corner of Church Street, the old barn shown in this picture used to provide a base for the Town Nightwatchman whose duty was to patrol the streets, calling the hours of darkness. The barn was demolished in 1888 to make way for the Salvation Army Citadel, opened in 1891, so the picture was taken no later than 1887. The tall building at the right became Stevens Drapery Store, then part of Brittain's.

30. Another advertising card, this time for Franks Furnishing Stores. In 1893 the firm were selling armchairs 'from 10s. 6d.' but this picture was taken later, in about 1900. The shop seems to have been emptied so as to display as many items as possible on the pavement. As well as leather chairs there were mattresses, tin trunks and a wickerwork push-chair. The shop was later taken over by Brittain's, along with Frank Stevens' property next door.

31. Mr. F. Brittain was issuing advertising cards too. This one displays his furniture van and members of his staff and family. The business was established in 1904 but this picture was taken in 1912, after the firm had moved from the Market Square to a small shop on the north side of the High Street and before their move to Franks's old shop.

32. From the tower of St. Neots church, the town looked like this in 1887. The High Street runs across the middle of the picture from left to right. The Old Meeting House with its pilastered front is visible because the Congregational Church was not built until 1888. The twin towers of the Methodist Church are at the right, behind the hipped roof of the building on the corner of Huntingdon Street. The Meeting House burnt down in the 1960's and the Methodist Church was pulled down.

33. The building at the left, on the corner of Huntingdon Street, was built in the 18th century as the George Inn with Assembly Rooms above. In about 1910, when the picture for this card was taken, Mr. Freeman had a grocery shop on the ground floor. This was later taken over by the Co-operative Society who eventually extended over the sites of the houses next to it and the Methodist Church.

34. Until the early part of this century these quaint little cottages stood on the west side of Huntingdon Street, at a point where Tebbutt's Road now goes through to link with New Street. The nearest one was a sweetshop kept by Chris Ashwell in the 1920's, when this picture was taken, but the advertisements suggest that it was also a general grocery shop.

35. On the east side of Huntingdon Street, this 18th century house occupied the site which became a garage, opposite the end of Bedford Street. It was lived in by a succession of well-to-do local families over the years and its grounds were used to accommodate the temporary huts of prisoners-of-war in World War Two. It was demolished in 1959. This picture, taken about 1930, shows why it was called Wisteria House.

36. All the buildings shown in this picture, taken about 1900, have now gone and are difficult to locate precisely. They stood at the upper end of Huntingdon Street near the Globe public house, in an area known to older residents as The Borough. These cottages appear to have been a conversion from a single hall house with cross wings, perhaps owned by a yeoman farmer of the 17th century.

PRIORY HILL AVENUE ST. NEOTS

37. Until the 1920's, Huntingdon Street was bare of buildings from The Borough to the Mill Lane crossroads with the fence of Priory Park on the right hand side. A right turn at the crossroads would have taken the traveller up this pleasant leafy lane in 1902, when this rather unseasonal postcard was issued to celebrate Christmas. The lane led up Priory Hill and at the top was the entrance to Priory Hill House.

St Neots, Road to Paper Mills.

38. From the top of Priory Hill the view was equally picturesque, looking back towards Mill Lane. Nowadays a wide roadway has replaced the cart track and only a handful of these fine old trees remain. Those on the right of this picture, which is on a card postmarked 1906, have all been felled and there is now a row of sodium street lights.

39. At the top of Priory Hill this pair of charming thatched cottages nestled among the trees and were comparatively new in about 1890, when this picture was taken. They had been built in the pseudo-rustic style much favoured by the Victorians and the occupants were gamekeepers who worked for the owner of Priory Hill House. They disappeared about 1950 or 1960.

40. A postcard of Priory Hill House as it was in 1930. The first house was built on the site in the 18th century but it was either altered or rebuilt in the 19th. Several generations of the Rowley family were born and died here. Their large private estate was acquired by the local Council in the 1960's and the house was demolished in 1965 to make way for a private housing estate. The fine parkland attached to the house then became a public open space.

41. In the 1930's the occupant of Priory Hill House was George Fydell Rowley who was noted for his eccentricities. He was violently opposed to motor-cars and expected his guests to arrive in horse-drawn vehicles or they were not invited again. His odd manner of dress and his habit of walking about the countryside with a rough stick are said to have led to him being mistaken for a tramp on several occasions. He became Lord of the Manor in 1902 and died in 1933.

42. A tributary of the Ouse called Henbrook runs between St. Neots and Eynesbury. The street beside it, on the St. Neots side, was known as Brook Side before it became Brook Street. This postcard of about 1905 shows the view looking east with St. Neots church tower in the background. To the right was a wharf where barges drew up to discharge and collect cargo, and opposite were the alehouses which served the needs of thirsty bargees. The White Swan is now a private house and the cottage next to it has gone.

Brook Side, St. Neots

43. Another card, posted in 1907, shows the wharf and the public houses more clearly. The Bushel and Strike in the foreground was at one time also a cheap lodging house with rather a bad reputation. The cottage between it and the White Swan was knocked down, widening the yard. At the time of the picture the yard led to yet another public house called the Bell.

44. On the same side of Brook Street as the wharf and a little beyond it were these cottages photographed in about 1902. They must have been very tiny, only one room wide. The space they occupied is now a grassed area leading to a wooden bridge over Henbrook and a pleasant riverside walk. The house at the extreme left became an opticians.

45. Further along the same side were more cottages in a similar style, photographed at the same time. They were knocked down to make a wider corner where Brook Street joins Church Street. The house next to them had its door partially bricked up and made into a window but Church House, nearest the camera, remains much the same.

46. This street was called New Lane in the 18th century so it is new only in relation to the Mediaeval streets such as Huntingdon Street. A postcard from 1910 gives a picture of what it was like before the Post Office was built beyond the Falcon on the left. In those days the Falcon did not open onto the street but had a garden in front of it.

NEW STREET, ST NEOTS.

47. In 1913 the Post Office moved to its present site in New Street. The gable end of the building can be seen on the left on this card posted in 1915. To the right the Wrestlers public house is still there, more tastefully decorated nowadays but without its ornate lamp bracket. Tebbutts Road now cuts through to Huntingdon Street beside the Baptist church.

New Street, St. Neots

48. A card posted in 1911 shows the spot more clearly. The elaborate gateway at the right led to the Baptist church and the railings beyond mark the point which is now the corner of Tebbutts Road. The writer of the card identified the lady as 'old Mrs. Ennals' and the gentleman in the background as the Reverend John Irvon Davies, the Congregational Church minister. The house at the left was once the home of the St. Neots Quadruplets, born in 1935.

St. Neots Paper Mills.

49. At the far end of New Street is Islands Common, an area of rough pasture over which grazing rights have existed since the Middle Ages. In 1908, when this card was posted, there were gates at both ends of the road across it. The road led to St. Neots Paper Mills which stood mainly on an island in the Ouse, with a few buildings on the further bank.

50. Beyond the top Common gate the road dips down and is subjected to frequent flooding from the river, so a raised walkway is provided for pedestrians. In 1905, about the time this picture was taken, the walkway, known locally as The Traps, was a wooden one. In recent years it has been rebuilt in concrete and steel and serves to protect walkers from traffic as well as floods.

51. On May 17th, 1912 there was a disastrous fire at the Paper Mills which destroyed many of the buildings completely and severely damaged the rest. Fire-engines were horse-drawn in those days and the equipment used was not sophisticated enough to cope with a really bad fire. Despite this setback the Mills were rebuilt in a remarkably short time and were in operation again in 1913.

From St Neots Spa

52. A view photographed in the 1890's shows the scene looking towards Little Paxton
from a part of the Paper Mills bridge called The Spa. The path on which the man was
standing was the old towpath for barges known as the Haling Way, 'haling' being an old
word for 'hauling'. The path has been cut away since then to widen the river but the track
at a higher level behind it remains as a public footpath.

53. A spring of mineral water, said to have medicinal properties, was discovered near the Paper Mills bridge in the late 19th century, and an enterprising local businessman established a well and an outlet on the site which he called The Spa. It was officially opened on June 3rd, 1895 and was marked by the procession of decorated boats shown in this photograph. Bottles of the water were also sold in local shops under the tradename Neotia.

625 CAMBRIDGE STREET, St. NEOTS

54. Running eastwards from the town centre is Cambridge Street. This postcard shows it in about 1920, before the building of Cambridge Gardens, which now lead off to the right from the region of the small cottage seen here. The shed in the centre of the picture, and the house to the right of it became a garage, and beyond that what was once a small café was later demolished and built further back from the road as a shop and restaurant.

55. This rural scene was the Kings Lane corner of Cambridge Street in about 1895. The footpath at the right and the little wooden footbridge are now a roadway and the stream runs almost unnoticed behind the garage and the houses that replaced the buildings on the left. The fields to the right and in the background are now covered with houses.

56. The name Green End indicates that this area, at the far end of Cambridge Street, was once a small hamlet, detached from the main town of St. Neots. This card was printed in about 1910 and the road has altered drastically since then. These cottages probably stood south of the road, near where the present Free Church is situated.

12. GREEN END. ST NEOTS.   COPYRIGHT

57. This card, posted in 1915, shows the same stretch of road from a point beyond the cottages. The present main Cambridge Road passes by to the left of this stretch, isolating it as a small lay-by. Behind the trees at the right was Shortsands House, later an old people's home. When this picture was taken the gap in the wall at the left led down some steps to a spring.

58. In the 1890's, when this photograph was taken, a long established footpath went from Cambridge Street through Rowley's Fields and round the south-eastern boundary of Priory Park to Priory Hill, with a branch leading from it going towards the station. Part of the route survives through alleyways from Cambridge Street to Almond Road, but the pretty rural stretch seen here has been swallowed up by a housing estate.

Station Hotel, St. Neots, Family & Commercial, Posting & Garage.

F. H. NICHOLS, PROPRIETOR.

59. St. Neots Railway Station was built in 1850, well out of town on the Cambridge Road at the insistence of Mr. Rowley. Opposite the station Mr. F.H. Nichols kept the Station Hotel and issued this advertising card in 1910. The station is still there but no hotel to cater for travellers. Opposite the line nowadays is an industrial estate, with factories and offices.

60. St. Neots has always been a town where people organised their own entertainment. In 1896 the group shown here was organised under the auspices of the Congretational Church, and was entitled 'The St. Neots United Pleasant Sunday Evening Band and Committee'. The President was the Reverend J.H. Harley and the Band was led by Mr. C. Brothers. There was also a Children's Choir.

61. There was a town band for many years as well, seen on this postcard wearing the smart uniforms which they wore in the 1920's, under the leadership of Mr. Harry Edwards. The first move to form a band was made in 1899 and by the 1900's The Eynesbury and St. Neots Brass Band was performing regularly at local fetes and sporting events. But musical tastes change and there is no longer a town band, although St. Neots has several societies catering for other kinds of music.

The Brook, St. Neots

62. The Eynesbury area, which became part of St. Neots in 1876, was slow to expand but its riverside area was commercially used from quite an early period. Rowing boats could be hired from the mooring shown on this card of about 1910, where tubs of flowers made an attractive landing stage. The backs of business premises in St. Neots are on the left. This area has been considerably altered to provide a Marina for private power boats.

63. The skyline of the main street of Eynesbury has changed very little from the view seen on this card of about 1900, but the ground floors have been altered and the old school in the foreground has been stripped of its plaster to show its half-timbering. A gap created by the demolition of a building about half-way down now leads to a small factory. The building at the far end of the left hand side of the street was then a public house called the Village Blacksmith.

St MARY'S STREET.
EYNESBURY. ST NEOTS.

A.E.J. Series No 3

St. Mary's Street, St. Neots

64. The shop on the left, seen here in about 1910, was knocked down in the 1960's in order to build a block of shops with flats above, but the new building blends well with the other property and retains Eynesbury's village character. When this picture was taken there were cottages down an alley to the left, in one of which James Toller had lived in the 18th century. He was known as the Eynesbury Giant because he grew to be 8 feet 6 inches tall.

Luke Street, Eynesbury, St. Neots.

65. Luke Street Eynesbury was a footpath from the Green to Montagu Square until it was built up in the late 19th century. This card of about 1920 shows workmen's cottages at the left and slightly larger terraced houses at the right, built in 1893. All these houses have now been smartened up and modernised and the street presents a pleasanter picture nowadays.

66. A view from Eynesbury Church tower, taken in 1889. In the background is St. Neots parish church and to its left the Congregational Church tower, built in 1888, but there is no sign of Paine's tower in Bedford Street, built in 1890. The long thin plots at the rear of the houses in St. Mary's Street stretch from left to right across the picture. There is now a cul-de-sac with new houses in it filling the plots beyond the greenhouses.

Eatonford, St. Neots

67. Across St. Neots bridge is Eaton Ford which became part of the town in 1965 along with Eaton Socon. In 1906, when this card was posted, the road from the bridge passed this row of cottages and Mr. Hite's grocery shop. Beyond them was a public house called the Rose and Crown, whose sign can be seen behind the pony trap. The public house and some of the cottages were demolished, the site then being used to display second-hand cars.

Eaton Ford, St. Neots

68. There were very few buildings round Eaton Ford Green when this card was posted in 1905, and very little traffic on the roads. To the left, beyond the buildings, was an area known as Weir Head. Houses now fill the gap to the right of the buildings and modern traffic requirements have meant road widening, eating into the Green, and the destruction of the fine row of trees to the right.

THE GEORGE BRIDGE, EATON SOCON.

69. Motorised transport arrived about 1910 and by 1916 Mr. Hinsby was running a local Motor Bus service. This card is from about that period. The bridge seen in the foreground has been widened and the brick parapet is now level with the front of the George and Dragon, so that many travellers are unaware that Duloe Brook passes under the road at this point. Nowadays Field Cottage Road leads off at the left, just beyond the bridge.

North Road, Eaton Socon.

70. The distant cars and the telegraph posts indicate that this card is also from about 1915. It is surprising to realise that this muddy, grass-edged track was the main Great North Road, later the A 1. The cottages at the left, already crumbling by then, have now gone and there are new housing estates off the main road on both sides.

Eaton Socon Village

71. About 1900, when this card appeared, there were no footpaths along the road's edge and not enough traffic to worry the pinafored children having their picture taken. The haircutter's shop is now a private house but the Waggon and Horses is still a public house although its sign had to be changed for a hanging one. On the other side of the road the white building became the Sun public house and shops were built beside it.

Eaton Socon Green

72. The buildings opposite Eaton Socon Green, as they appeared on a postcard written in 1907. The Wheatsheaf public house on the left is the only building which remains the same. Some properties were rebuilt between the wars, others more recently, and a housing estate now backs on to part of this frontage too. Road widening has whittled away part of the Green and a War Memorial was erected on it after World War One.

73. Eaton Socon was famous at one time for its May Day celebrations and a tall maypole was a permanent feature on the Green until it was blown down in a gale in 1915. This card, dated 1912, shows children from the village school taking bows and making curtseys after performing a dance that involved sword-play by the boys. The large audience in the background testifies to the popularity of these events, which unhappily no longer take place.

SWEEPS & MILKMAID DANCE. EATON SOCON.

74. Another traditional ritual was the Sweeps and Milkmaids dance, also performed on May Day at Eaton Socon. This card is dated 1907. It is probable that the sweeps with their sooty faces were the natural successors to the black-faced mummers of the past, and milkmaids were associated with Flora, a pagan goddess. In recent years St. Neots Folk Club dancers have revived this traditional dance and they perform it on May Day mornings.

75. The Cage in School Lane, Eaton Socon, was built as the village 'lock-up', as its heavily studded door demonstrates. This card shows it before restoration and with the old primary school, now demolished, in the background. One of the posters on the wall advertised a Dance and Fete at Eynesbury at which the Blue Hungarian Band would be playing and the London Bioscope Company would show films. The date was Tuesday, September 8th, 1908.

1843 The Green and War Memorial, Eaton Socon

76. This final picture postcard shows Eaton Socon Green in about 1928. The row of houses facing the camera have now been rebuilt and Mr. Townsend's shop at the right has gone, along with the other buildings. The signs of changes which would come in the 1930's are seen here. The motor car in the middle distance foreshadows the constant hubbub of modern traffic and the War Memorial foreshadows the Second World War while it commemorates the First.